T0354382

TEMPTATION

PATSY F. HAMIL

Order this book online at www.trafford.com
or email orders@trafford.com

Most Trafford titles are also available at major online book retailers.

Print information available on the last page.

ISBN: 978-1-6987-1122-5 (sc)
ISBN: 978-1-6987-1121-8 (hc)
ISBN: 978-1-6987-1120-1 (e)

Library of Congress Control Number: 2022903712

All scripture passages are taken from the King James Version of the Holy Bible.
Webster's Ninth New Collegiate Dictionary

Trafford rev. 02/28/2022

 www.trafford.com
North America & international
toll-free: 844-688-6899 (USA & Canada)
fax: 812 355 4082

Special thank you to

Trafford Publishing Team
Kevin Raines for publishing assistance
Mary Israel for computer assistance
Gina Raines for art work
Haley Walker for silhouette
Kyli Putzek for computer assistance

CONTENTS

CONTENTS

PREFACE

This book is written for new Christians and those who seek a deeper relationship with Christ. It was composed through prayer, meditation, and by the grace and power of our Lord in spite of spiritual conflict and the hindrances of Satan. The life thrilling experiences are true and are recorded for the exaltation of God our Father, who is over all and above all in heaven and on earth. Praise is given for the glory of God.

I am dedicating this book to my wonderful family and in memory of my loving husband, Jimmy, who taught me about salvation through Jesus, which in turn changed my life and my lifestyle.

I am grateful for the encouragement that my daughter, Jodie, gave me and for her great faith in serving God even through many trials and persecutions.

In the year of our Lord 2000
Patsy F. Hamil

Matthew 6:13 And lead us not into temptation, but deliver us from evil: for thine is the kingdom, and the power, and the glory, forever. Amen.

OUR SOVEREIGN GOD

On a cool, brisk autumn morning, quietness covers the land; and trees bow with obeisance in the presence of the Almighty God. It is He that hath made the seasons and beautified the earth with splendor. Herbs of the field lift up a wave offering as the day breaks with a gentle flowing breeze. Fragrant flowers adorned with magnificence pay reverence to their creator.

His words created the glittering stars and planets and uniquely set them into space. The sun and the moon in appropriate settings divided the light from the darkness. As I look upon this earth and into the heavens, I see the handiwork of God and stand amazed at His greatness.

The peace I feel in my heart as I begin to know Him in the spirit passes all understanding. Gentle as a dove, He abides within to guide and direct my paths into righteousness. As I read and study His word, my faith extends to deeper and greater depths. I begin to experience the hidden mysteries of my Maker.

His peaceful nature as gentle waters trickling over smooth stones in a nearby brook can be powerfully transformed into a jealous and angry God unleashing His wrath upon the sins of this world. As blusterous clouds roll across the sky, I acknowledge and am made aware of the only true God who has control over heaven and earth. His voice rumbles like thunder. His finger transmits lightning to split the east from the west. One breath can make the mountains crumble into minute grains of sand and can part the deepest sea. The earth trembles and quakes at the mere mention of His name. The omnipotent, all-powerful, unlimited God can become a consuming fire. The winds violently cyclone across the desert seeking destruction and yet obey His voice when He speaks: "Peace, be still."

The angels bow before Him, not only on earth but also in heaven, crying, "Holy, holy, holy, Thou art worthy, the Most High who was and is and will be forever and ever the Alpha and Omega, the beginning and the end." The acceptance of Him and His creation is not to be mocked or looked upon as a mere coincidence of nature or a big bang, for He is the Great I Am.

As you begin your journey into the realms of spirituality, behold the majesty of our Lord. Seek the wisdom of our Creator, for He alone can help you find your destiny. Do not take

Him frivolously. He has the authority to cast your body and soul into hell for eternity.

Come with me as we take our steps together from salvation to the Holy Ghost's power.

CHAPTER 1

AFTER SALVATION—
THEN WHAT?

Salvation is a spiritual quest and a wonderful gift from God. It is by faith, "the substance of things hoped for, the evidence of things not seen" (Heb. 11:1), that you become saved. It is not by works (Eph. 2:8-9), doing good deeds, or by having a good moral character. It is only by faith in the crucifixion and resurrection of Jesus that you can be born again. Salvation is for all with no respect of persons and for whosoever will believe. The acceptance or rejection determines the ultimate fate of your soul for eternity. Acceptance is such a celebrated occasion that there is joy in the presence of the angels when a soul is saved and a name is written in the Lamb's Book of Life. God's amazing grace brings divine favor and goodwill accompanied by the precious Holy Spirit to lead, guide, and sustain you.

After salvation, you become a son or daughter of the Most High and a joint heir of a kingdom not made by hands. You are a new creature in Christ. Old things have passed away and behold all things have become new (2 Cor. 5:17). You have been promoted from a poor lost sinner to a wealthy King's kid. A crown of life, a new immortal body, and a heavenly mansion is waiting at the end of your journey. Your sins have been forgiven and forgotten. It's as though you have just been born, and now you have a new start in life. You have become a full-pledged runner in a race for a crown of life. You are standing on the solid rock of Christ Jesus, and the gates of hell cannot prevail against it

(Matt.16:18). This rock will never crumble or erode, and it will withstand the turbulent winds of Satan and the torrential rains that beat against it.

Instead of practicing evil works such as adultery, fornication (sex before marriage), uncleanness, idolatry, witchcraft, hatred, jealousy, arguing, strife, wrath, murder, drunkenness, etc. (Gal. 5:19–21), you should now bear the fruits of the spirit which are love, joy, peace, long-suffering, gentleness, goodness, faith, meekness, and temperance or self-control (Gal. 5:22–23). Set your goals to be Christlike, for Christians are God's hands and feet, and His way of spreading the good news to mankind.

A good way to begin your new life is by confessing that Jesus is Lord. He has become your Savior, and now it is time to make Him Lord of your life. Don't be ashamed publicly, but acknowledge what He has done for you.

Read Romans 1:16 about how He has changed your life. You will be the only Bible some people read, and they will watch you closely. You will be a light in a world of darkness. Shine that you may lead someone to know redemption. Take any opportunity to give your testimony and share the gospel with someone. A person who wins souls is wise (Prov. 11:30).

Even though you have just started your walk with the Lord, the devil won't waste any time hindering you. One way he agitates your mind is by reminding you of your past sins and what a failure you were. If you listen to him, regret will stunt your spiritual growth by keeping you in the stage of repentance and never moving forward. As long as you remain whining about your past, you are no threat to him, and you cannot be a vibrant servant of God. Remember, once you ask God to forgive you for your sins, He forgives and forgets about them. Don't look back but look upward to Christ. It's all right to remember your past, but think of it in a positive way. God brought you out of your sins. He has loosened the chains of bondage and set you free. You have been redeemed and are standing on higher ground. Don't make the mistake of stepping back into the sinking sand. Go forward in your Christian walk holding on to God's hand. Philippians 4:13 says, "I can do all things through Christ which strengtheneth me."

After salvation, you become a babe in Christ, and now the growing process starts. Just like a newborn baby needs milk, you must first start with the basics:

THE FIRST STEP IS PRAYER

Prayer is how you communicate with or talk to your Heavenly Father. As you know, he loves you with a perfect unconditional love. Accept His love and love Him in return by telling Him your every thought and care. He is concerned with every detail in your life no matter how insignificant it may seem. Every incident is important to God. Acknowledge Him in all your ways, and He will direct your path (Prov. 3:6). Greeting Him in prayer at daybreak or when you first arise from sleep is a good way to start your day in a positive manner. If you don't know how to pray, He gave you a good example in the Word known as the Lord's Prayer (Matt. 6:9–13). The more you pray, the easier it will become. Just talk to God as you do to another person. He is not interested in gallant intellectual speeches, but he wants to hear what is in your heart. He knows your intent even before you speak. There is no need to be embarrassed or ashamed to talk to God for you are beginning a new relationship and allowing Him to become your Father. Even though you may not see Him visibly, you can feel His presence and know that He is real. He listens and hears when you pray. "For the eyes of the Lord are over the righteous, and His ears are open unto their prayers" (1 Pet. 3:12). As you progress in your prayer life, you will find that you can have a prayer in your heart and mind throughout the day as the Bible teaches us to pray without ceasing (1 Thess. 5:17). You will find that prayer becomes a subconscious thought as well as a conscious one. If you do this, the devil will have a difficult time sneaking in to steal your joy. Keep your guard up! Don't give the devil a chance! Fill your mind with positive thoughts and things that are true, honest, just, pure, and of good report (Phil. 4:8). There will be no room for gloom, despair, or agony, which can hinder your walk with God.

When you pray, acknowledge who God is and have a grateful heart. Give him praise for His goodness, mercy, and for all the blessings He has given you. He gave us eternal life through His only Son and supplies our every need. The Bible teaches us to be thankful *in* all things not *for* all things (1 Thess. 5:18). Sometimes hard times come to everyone, and bad things happen to good people. Praying to God can help you through the tough times, knowing that He is always with you. God knows and cares, and He wants a relationship with you. He has a great plan for your life. Even though there may be times when you think that God doesn't hear your prayers or that He doesn't answer when you pray, remember and trust that He does hear and He has the right answer. Pray according to His will and not your own. Sometimes you may only look at the circumstances, but He looks at the solution. We make plans for our lives but ask God to direct the steps we need to take. Just because we make our own plans doesn't mean our plan is in His will. Remember His thoughts are higher than our thoughts, and His ways are perfect. God works miracles in our lives, and His timing is perfect.

THE SECOND STEP IS THE WORD

The Word or the Bible was inspired by the Holy Ghost that you might have a guideline or instructions on how to live a victorious life. Jesus came that we might have life and have it more abundantly (John 10:10). As you read and study, the Holy Spirit will reveal the meaning of the Word and will bring the scriptures to your remembrance to enable you to resist sin. The Bread of Life becomes meat for your soul. The deeper you reach into the Word, the stronger your spiritual walk will become. This will be a daily growth. You can't learn it all in one day. As a matter of fact, you will never know it all. We do not have the mind of God, and we only gaze through a glass dimly, but the Spirit of God can assist us in learning and seeing things more clearly.

After hearing or reading the Word, you may experience growing pains in your spirit, for the Word is like a two-edged sword (Heb. 4:12).

Sometimes it cuts deeply into the heart and may even hurt your feelings. This is a spiritual purging. Purging cleanses and purifies your heart that you might bear fruit. A parable in the Bible describes Christians as being branches and Jesus being the true vine (John 15:1–6). Unless the branches of a fruit tree are pruned or trimmed, the tree cannot produce fruit plentifully. The Word purges or teaches you how to cut away the sins and strongholds that have attached to your life so they won't cause you to wither from the vine. You cannot face Satan unless you stay attached to the vine, for Jesus is your strength and source of power. Even though you experience growing pains or take personal notice when the preacher or pastor speaks words that prick your heart, don't get offended or discouraged or think he is singling you out of the congregation. A God-called minister only preaches what God leads him to say, and it reaches all ears that listen. The

Word rebukes and reproves but also encourages and instructs to keep you on the road to righteousness. As an earthly father corrects his children, God also corrects His children by the Word. His Word is good and powerful.

If you stumble or fall, get up and try again. Everyone makes mistakes and will continue to as long as life exists on earth. There was only one that was perfect and that was Jesus Christ (Heb. 4:15). All of us have sinned and come short of the glory of God (Rom. 3:23)

Since the day of Adam, man has obtained the knowledge of good and evil. It is up to you whether you will be victorious or become a coward and run away in defeat. God has given you a commander in chief (the Holy Spirit) to walk with you and direct your path to victory. Though you may face the enemy head-on, you have the equipment and armor to stand (Eph. 6:13–17). Clothe yourself with the whole armor of God and be equipped with weapons for battle and protection. Be prepared to meet opposition for you will encounter resistance from demonic powers in a world of evil and darkness. Do not be alarmed for the Lord has overcome the world. Satan can only growl and place stumbling blocks in front of you, but Jesus has all power over him. Stand still and see what God can do. Make these stumbling blocks stepping-stones and walk on top of the devil. Learn from your mistakes and don't keep making the same ones. Jesus will forgive you, but He says, "Go and sin no more" (John 8:11). Therefore, repent and charge onward as a Christian soldier in battle.

The Word is a lamp unto your feet and a light unto your path (Ps. 119:105). Through the Holy Spirit, God has given you a lamp trimmed and burning. Keep your lamp filled with the Holy Ghost's power for the further you go in your race, the more power you will need. Stay on the straight path in front of you for straight is the gate, and narrow is the way that leads to life. Do not turn or detour on the road that leads to destruction which has a wide gate and a broad way where many will go therein (Matt. 7:13–14). Even though you will encounter obstacles and traps, God will never leave you nor forsake you. You will never be tempted beyond tolerance without being provided a means of escape.

Since we wrestle against principalities and powers of darkness and not against flesh and blood (Eph. 6:12), a spiritual battle may become tiring and require a great effort of spiritual strength. You may be weak, but Jesus is strong. Learn to lean on Him and let Him carry you when times are hard and burdens become too heavy. You may be perplexed but not in despair, persecuted but not forsaken, cast down but not destroyed (2 Cor. 4:8–9). When trouble comes, remember God's promise that all things work together for good to them that love Him, to them who are called according to His purpose (Rom. 8:28), so don't lose faith but keep holding on.

THE THIRD BASIC STEP IS TO ASSEMBLE WITH BELIEVERS AND ATTEND CHURCH

We read in Hebrews 10:25 to forsake not the assembling of yourselves together as the manner of some is but to be among God's people. You will draw strength and faith by worshipping together. Being alone can put a damper on your growth spiritually and can provide an opportune time for Satan to converse with you. As you recall in Luke 4, Jesus was alone in the wilderness and was tempted by Satan (however, to no avail). Being with fellow believers enables you to share your experiences, and you can bind together in faith. If you have faults, confess them one to another. If you have problems, share your burdens and pray one for another.

Talk to someone you can trust and confide in someone who may have gone through the same situation as you. Solitude is a trap for loneliness, and burdens can become too heavy to bear alone. Give them to God and let Him carry the load for he knows how to handle the situation without fail. Keep communication open to one another and unto God and be an overcomer by your testimony.

As on the day of Pentecost (Acts 2:1–4) being in one mind and one accord can open the door to spiritual levels of praise and growth. God inhabits the praises of His people and in return pours out blessings that you cannot even contain. There is strength and happiness as you join together in heavenly places. Singing glorious melodies to God blesses Him and fills your soul with exceeding joy as a well springing up that never runs dry, bubbling with freshness and holiness with adoration to the honor of God.

Bible studies, Sunday schools, training hours, and fellowship are good filling stations that will boost your faith and will be a good time for learning and sharing. Finding a spirit-filled Bible-believing church enables you to grow and to please God. Become a part of it. Worshipping together lets God know how much you love Him and one another.

THE FOURTH BASIC STEP IS BAPTISM

Baptism will not save you, but it is a willing step of surrender to God and His will. Jesus was baptized by John, and God spoke these words: "This is my beloved son in whom I am well pleased." We please God when we show that our hearts have been changed. As we go down into the water, we are signifying that the old man (the sinner) is being buried. As we come up out of the water, it symbolizes that our sins are washed away by the blood of the Lamb, and a new man (saved by grace through faith) has come forth.

If you are able physically to be baptized, don't let anything hinder you from this act of faith and acknowledgment of salvation. You will be blessed for your obedience.

THE FIFTH BASIC STEP IS BEING RESPONSIBLE

As you sanctify or cleanse yourself with the Word and now associate with believers, it is time for step 5. It is necessary to separate yourself from the world or fleshly desires. The Bible teaches us to lay aside every weight and sin that so easily besets us (Heb. 12: 1-2). If you had a weakness for alcohol, drugs, sex, fighting, gambling, cheating, lying, stealing, etc., when you were an unbeliever, you should stay away from environments that would be a hindrance or temptation to you. Don't test your self-control. You might find that your willpower is weaker than you think. You alone are not even a contestant when it comes to rivalry with Satan. Only through faith, the Word, and God's grace are you able to stand firm for Jesus. Satan knows your weaknesses as well as God and will inflict you with arrows of persuasion. Remember, he is out to deceive and lie to you (John 8:44) for the wages of sin is death, and after death the judgment. There is pleasure in sin for a season, and Satan will portray a beautiful setting of glamour and excitement but will fail to reveal the entanglement and destructive results. Satan only comes to kill, steal, and destroy (John 10:10).

The Bible teaches us to keep ourselves unspotted from the world and without blemish or sin. You can do this only with God's help, and take it a day at a time. God has already won the battle, and the devil is a defeated foe. Jesus is victorious with the power of resurrection, and since this power has come to dwell in you (for your body is the temple of the Holy Ghost I Cor. 6:19), you too can become victorious. You too can have power over sin through the blood that Jesus shed for you on Calvary. You can become more than a conqueror.

The choices you make in life are left up to you. You are the one who chooses. Whether you choose to follow God's teaching or whether you choose to serve Satan is up to you. If you make the wrong decision, you cannot place the blame on anyone, not even the devil. He only offers, and you make the choice to accept the temptation or refuse it. Responsibility may be a difficult task, but it's a necessity in your spiritual growth. Take time in making decisions and pray for wisdom and guidance. God is omnipresent and is available at all times whenever or wherever you call. He will lead you in the way of righteousness if you will heed His voice and harden not your heart.

As you grow spiritually, you will learn to be a doer of the word and not a hearer only (James 1:22). Faith comes by hearing, and faith is led by God's instruction. Doing is faith put into action and it is followed by results. Faith without works is dead, being alone (James 1:17). If you do not put action with your faith, how can you show others that you believe? God is unhappy with a slothful or lazy servant but blesses the one who is busy and about His work. There are so many souls to reach and so few laborers.

God is a jealous God and distinctly commands you to put Him first in your life. "Thou shall have no other gods before me" (Exod. 20:3). If you follow His commandments, He will supply all of your need according to His riches in glory. As you work for Him, you will reap many benefits. God gives us duties, and as good stewards, we should obey. His Work tells us that obedience is better than sacrifice (1

Sam. 15:22). One way to show your trust and obedience to God is by bringing your tithes and offerings into the church (Mal. 3:8-12). He will open the windows of heaven and pour out blessings that there shall not be room enough for you to receive. You and what you have will be blessed. Give and it shall be given unto you; good measure pressed down, and shaken together, and running over, shall men give into your bosom (Luke 6:38). No need for worry or fretting for your life is in the hands of God. If He feeds the sparrow and clothes the lilies of the field, how much more will He do for you?

The growth in your spiritual walk depends on your dedication to *prayer*, studying the Word, *baptizing*, praising and *assembling* together, sanctification, and accepting *responsibility*.

As you follow these basic steps, the process of growth will come naturally as you seek a deeper relationship with God.

Whatever you choose to do, to grow or turn back, remember whatsoever a man sows, that shall he also reap—corruption or life everlasting (Gal. 6:7–8). Records are being kept, and rewards will come. Therefore, store up rewards for the good works that you do for God and don't let your rewards be burned as stubble. Our choices end in blessings or curses. Living for God is a gratifying and wonderful life on earth. Stay on the firing line and the battlefield for the Lord. You can be victorious through Him.

SILHOUETTE ARTWORK
BY: HAILEY WALKER

CHAPTER 2
TEMPTATION

In the beginning, the world was a paradise of peace and tranquility, and mankind was made in the likeness and image of God. Through His breath, man became a living soul.

As animals roamed freely, no rival was instigated between man and beast. In the cool of the day, man walked and conversed with God, having fellowship and closeness as a potter with his clay. He ate the fruit of the land and toiled not. No pain or sorrow had entered into the heart of man. No disease had transpired, and the only fear was the admiration of the Lord. Man was at peace with creation and with the Creator. Naked walked he before God. No money or medium of exchange was essential for God had made provision for all needs.

Authority and dominion were designated to man, and it was good in the sight of the Lord. As the days of creation were completed, man and woman inhabited the earth, and human beings began to experience life. Through God's love for man, instructions and directions were given in the Garden of Eden, and God gave mankind a will of his own.

Since Lucifer had been cast out of heaven's portals with his attempt to become most high as God, he took advantage at this time to use his cunning ability of deception to proposition Eve with contrary statements concerning God's instruction. Eve hesitated and listened to Satan, which was the first mistake. The initial step of choice between obedience and disobedience evolved. Obedience to God is the act of acknowledging and displaying submission toward His will. Since God has a perfect will and does not waver, being a Christian, we should adhere to His leadership. Adam and Eve had a choice to follow God's will or a choice of self-will. Sadly, their choice changed the whole course of God's wonderful and perfect plan. Their choice has affected every soul of man that has been conceived since that time. We now are born into sin, and every man has to give an account of his life unto God.

Anytime man permits self-pleasure or fulfillment of the flesh to enter, it leads to spiritual dissension. If we allow Satan to enter our minds and then ponder upon his insidious lies, we open the door to destruction and death. Satan, like the serpent, slithers secretly and quietly into the mind; and if you let him linger or abide, doubt and confusion are born, and sin commences.

As deception started in the day of Adam, it is rampant today on the job, at home, in school, in politics, and in the church. Since the devil goes to and fro seeking whom he may devour, location doesn't matter. If you think you are hidden and are safe from his snares in the church, you are deceiving yourself. Temptations of jealousy, envy, strife, gossiping, and backbiting are only a few of the demons that scamper about whispering in your ear. Compass the margins of your mind with the Word to restrain the trespasses of the devil for he can only do what you allow him to do. By the Word, the progression of temptation has to decline or take another course of action. You can deter his plan and make his corruption difficult. It is better to deal with him at the first moment you sense his presence than to grow weary in the battle. You have the power in the name of Jesus if you will use it.

At times we tend to allow temptation to rule us tyrannically by wanting to work it out ourselves or thinking that we have it under control. Don't sell the devil short, for without God, we could not go against him or his demonic power. We do not have the strength or knowledge to face him alone. His craftiness and beguiling nature will carry us off course and send us on a path of damnation. Sin will build a pyramid and will become a tomb of desolate sorrow. The way of escape can only be through the Lord Jesus and His Word.

There are innumerable temptations that we face daily; therefore, be sober and discipline yourself to recognize when Satan presents one for the taking.

Notice three main areas of temptation that prevail in the world (1 John 2:16): *lust of the flesh*, *lust of the eyes*, and the *pride of life*.

Let's start with the *lust of the flesh* and take a look at what Satan offers and the destructive road he can lead you down.

The desire of the flesh is controversial, and many people dispute views on this topic, but God has spoken plainly through His Word that he who commits adultery, fornication, or acts of uncleanness will not inherit the kingdom of God (Gal. 5:19). Beware of the deception that Satan uses to blind mankind. It is true that God made the body beautiful and pleasing to the eyes, but if you recall in Genesis, after Adam and Eve sinned, they hid from God, being ashamed that they were naked. Enticing mankind with nakedness is a deception that develops into fornication and adultery. The flesh always desires pleasure.

Over a period of time, sex has gradually crept into the field of advertisement. Throughout the world, it is being used to promote the sale of goods. Manufacturers are becoming wealthy through the means of sexual illustrations. Emphasis on sex heightens the sale of makeup, food, sports, movies, clothing, music, etc. In past years, what was censored for radio and television is no longer considered immoral. Publications to entice or arouse the desire of the flesh are being magnified. We have allowed Satan to progress slowly by compromising and accepting these temptations as a fad, trend, or just being a part of life. Christians have stood idle and have not held up the high standard and banner of Christ. Morals have declined, and sin has corrupted mankind. God is the same yesterday, today, and forever; and sin is sin no matter who committed it and when it is committed. A reckoning day is coming, and every person on the face of the earth, dead or alive, will stand before the judgment of God.

Everyone likes to be needed or wanted by someone. This is not sinful if you remain within the boundaries of God's will. Marriage was made for man and woman who could not contain themselves and to avoid fornication (1 Cor. 1:7). Sex before marriage is fornication. Just because it feels good or is exciting doesn't make it right in the sight of God. A marriage certificate makes a difference. If a person yields to the temptation and desire of the flesh outside of God's will, he or she will become a target for Satan to manifest himself.

Lust of the flesh starts early in life; and unless parents teach their children the ways of the Lord, innocence and purity will be lost and become a thing of the past. Hormonal changes develop, and the desire for the "sense of touch" gets stronger.

After the experience of kissing and petting, young ladies and young men find that their emotions begin to rage high and soon find themselves out of control. One step follows another, and the innocence and youthful purity of virginity are lost in a matter of minutes. It is replaced by a wounded conscience that wishes it hadn't happened. Guilt and shame will escalate, and there is no way to go back and start over. There is no way to turn the tide, and sorrowful memories can linger for a lifetime.

Children of today are being deceived into accepting sexual freedom. The world teaches that if it feels right, do it. Education teaches that it's all right if you use condoms for protection or some type of birth control, or solve the problem by abortion. This is not God's way or His teaching, and it is an abomination to the Lord. The world's way is God's enemy and only leads to damnation.

As the world promotes these ungodly standards with no rules, people will soon begin to accept the ways of man and not God. Man will begin to justify their ways and will have no boundaries. Without good morals and guidelines, anyone can do whatever and whenever they want.

When sexual temptation comes and when God speaks to your heart through the Holy Spirit, listen to that still small voice. The Holy Spirit will guide and lead you the right way. Make the right choice. If you do not listen and push godly thoughts to the back of your mind and let the flesh rule, you then choose to be selfish, and your desires will override your spirit. The natural desires of man and woman will cunningly turn into a sensual, passionate, and pleasure-seeking vessel that will soon increase an appetite wanting more to quench its thirst.

One time won't be enough. The temptation will come again and more often. Each time will be easier, and God's voice will be quieter as you push Him away. Your conscience will become seared, and soon it won't bother you at all to have a sexual partner. It will seem like a natural and normal thing to do. You make the choice to listen to God or listen to Satan. Be strong in the Lord and learn to say no to Satan and yes to Jesus.

I'm sure you've heard people say one thing leads to another. This is true. If Satan can bind you with one stronghold, he will have another stronghold waiting for you. Pornography, phone sex, and promiscuity can weave a web of fantasy and pleasure. Sexual sins, if practiced and not stopped, become the initial base for molestation, rape, incest, homosexuality, sodomy, venereal diseases, etc. Children, the elderly, and the innocent become victims of horrendous acts that can impair and destroy their lives forever. Prisons are overfilled with rampant raging men and women who have allowed Satan to destroy their minds and have transformed them into murderous, psychotic puppets. They have lost their fear of God and have no regard for life. Some are controlled by demonic forces and are damned for eternity. This is not God's will.

God wishes that all would come to repentance and that none should perish.

Being single is a good thing. Having a friend or companion can be a blessing without having an intimate sexual relationship. You can be happy if you have a relationship with God. If you put God first, then you can have a fulfilled life. Believe it or not, you don't have to have sex to live. Food and water are requirements, but not sex. We were born to worship God, so if you get your priorities in order, you can be happy and have peace within.

I'm not saying don't ever marry. In fact, I'll admit that I have been married twice—once in the flesh and once in God. The flesh didn't last. That's one reason I can write to you now because I have experienced being a sinner and later becoming a Christian. I know the pros and cons, and being a Christian and finding who God wants you to have as a soul mate is a better choice. Being equally yoked, both being

Christians seeking to do God's will makes life a whole lot easier. It's not a bed of roses all the time, but God will help you if you put Him first and seek His guidance.

God's way of love in a marriage is a beautiful love. Sex doesn't have to be evil, but it can be good. The Bible teaches us that the bed is undefiled in marriage. Giving yourself to one another in love is gratifying and also keeps your relationship with one another strong. God intended for it to be this way in order for us to multiply and replenish the earth. Your companion can be all you need, plus be your best friend. If Satan tempts you with an attraction for another person, talk to your companion about the temptation and keep your thoughts out in the open. Communication between a husband and wife is to be shared.

When you were united in marriage, you became one. There shouldn't be a fear between you and your spouse that would cause any conflict. You should be able to talk about everything together without putting a strain on your relationship. You should be honest with each other and trust each other. Being tempted by someone else is not a discredit to your marriage. A true Christian husband or wife will take time to listen and will understand that no one is exempt from temptation. The temptation itself is not the sin, but it is the acceptance of the temptation and the application of it to your life that becomes the sin.

Talk about the temptation, and then pray about it together. When you hide thoughts from your spouse, it gives Satan a chance to deepen your thoughts. Evil thinking or lustful thoughts can take root. Since Satan is the power of darkness, he likes to keep things in secret or behind closed doors in darkness. Jesus is the light, and He opens our eyes to let us see the deception.

God took a rib from Adam's side to form Eve, so stand side by side in your marriage and encourage one another in the pure love of God. There will be no room for jealousy to slip in if you confide in one another. Be friends and not just lovers. Trust grows and faithfulness flourishes as your closeness binds you together when you share every aspect of life. Your love will grow deeper and stronger.

If you fail to love with godly love, jealousy will rule and harsh criticism from your mate will only antagonize and intimidate. Hurt will turn into anger, and the love you once shared will be demolished, and subsequently, mental and physical abuse ignites. Disgust and hatred take the place of love and comfort. Domestic violence, pain, and sorrow replace peace, contentment, and joy. The abuse can be prevented if you listen and follow God's will.

God has such a wonderful plan for man and woman to have a beautiful relationship and a loving family if you don't allow ignorance and disobedience to enter. So many times, we open doors for stressful situations that could be avoided by the help of God through prayer. Let's forget "my way" and do it "God's way." Considering your spouse and their feelings before your own will lead to a healthy, beautiful relationship. "Me, myself, and I" are selfish motives and set a standard for destruction.

If you choose not to live by the commandments of God and you both do not follow His teachings but live in the flesh, sexual desires can result in adultery, and adultery to divorce. The results of lust can destroy relationships, families, children, and friends. Sinful desires become the basic grounds for needless pain and heartache. Hadn't you rather follow God and enjoy His blessings and benefits?

Lust of the flesh not only means sex, it can also mean anything that is enjoyable to your flesh such as alcohol, drugs, food, etc. Any addiction to the flesh can become a chain of bondage. It can become your god. Satan does not show you the consequences of these lusts. He lets you indulge in the high feeling or the satisfaction it gives you for a moment. He doesn't show you the future result of torture, disfigurement, and distortion of your body and mind. He doesn't reveal the captivity and dependence and the fact that you become a slave to your desire and lose control of your own body.

You have the power to overcome if you will be obedient to the Holy Spirit's convicting power. This power is for your benefit. Make wise decisions instead of hasty emotional judgments. If someone offers you drugs, alcohol, or sex, abstain from it. Walk away and smile. Take time to listen to God's voice and live a blessed life.

Secondly, let's look at the temptation of the lust of the eyes. The Bible tells us in Matthew

5:28 that if you look upon a woman (or man) to lust after her (or him), you commit adultery in your heart. You may say, "How can you not look if a beautiful female or handsome male just happens to come your way?" This scripture does not mean that you have to wear blinders or keep your head down and not look at anyone. No, this only means not to hold on to the temptation and give it time to grow roots. Recognition of someone's looks is not the sin. When you dwell on it after the temptation enters your mind and let it abide in your heart till it becomes a fantasy or obsession, then it becomes sin. Clean your thoughts, submit yourself to God, resist the devil, and he will flee from you.

There are many temptations of the eyes other than sexual lust. Lust for things can build up to covetousness. We see a lot, and we want a lot. Material possessions are so readily available that temptation does not have to be too strong for us to accept it willingly. *Wants* and *needs* are two different words and have two different meanings. God supplies our needs according to His riches in glory. The discretion of our wants is left up to us. The Bible teaches us to lay up treasures in heaven where moth and rust don't corrupt and where thieves do not break through nor steal (Matt. 6:21). Where your treasure is, there will your heart be also.

A lot of times, we develop a financial disaster by wanting things that are above our means. The devil entices with material possessions and with the easy credit card we tend to over-limit our budget. Sometimes we stretch our income to the penny by buying things that we could easily do without. The devil takes notice when we do this, and he sends sickness our way or mechanical trouble with our vehicles, or some unexpected expense. Resorting to more bank loans seems to be the solution, but monthly payments and interest keep building. Usually, our income has no more elasticity, and after a lengthy struggle, it sometimes results in bankruptcy or a bad credit record.

To the devil's delight, we have fallen into his trap, and he stands by laughing at our dilemma. His presentation of how enjoyable something would be will blind you to the actual fact that you have to pay for it or suffer the consequences. Financial burdens produce tension and excessive demands on marriages and families. Debt can promote stress, mental oppression, and health issues. A lot of times, the inevitability to cope with the strain and pressure of indebtedness ends in an attempt at suicide, and in some cases, precious life is wasted in fatality.

Sin spreads and divides into many aspects and can stretch from stealing to imprisonment. Things by themselves are not sin, but the love for them can possess all your time and can become your god. Coveting in return births idolatry. Anything that pushes God to the background is sin. A lot of times, this is not willfully done; but in ignorance, we tend to get our minds so fixed upon things we want that we call on God only when something goes wrong or some catastrophe takes place. Idols do not have to be statues made of gold or silver. They can be anything you let take the place of God. Television, music, sports, shopping, etc., are only a few methods of time consumption. The list is unlimited. If you are not careful, these things will become priorities and habit forming. You will be too busy to find time to pray, study, or attend church.

God's plan is for us to be a blessed people. He has provided an assurance of an abundant life if we are willing to be obedient to His Word and follow His will. We can be prosperous in health and welfare if we will trust and believe. He is true and faithful to His promises. He will provide, and His grace is sufficient for all our needs. We limit God so many times by not seeking His guidance and wisdom in our actions. He has what we need if we will only ask according to His will. We have not because we ask not, or we ask amiss. We must first ask, seek, and knock (Matt. 7:7), and the answers and solutions will be given, found, and opened. If you learn to keep your focus on Jesus, you can prevent a lot of disasters from happening. The Bible teaches us to seek first the kingdom of God and all these things will be added unto you. If you delight yourself in the Word and keep his commandments, He will give you the desires of your heart. You will have more to share and bless others.

Your mind is the most complicated yet most delicate source of power of the body. The way you think constitutes how your day will progress. The saying "We create our own sunshine as well as our own clouds" has pertinent meaning. Isn't it strange that if someone tells you that you don't look well, before the end of the day, you will dwell on that thought and will feel sick by the power of their suggestion. I believe the encouraging words from the Bible that tell us to think of good things and good reports are stated for a good reason. Positive thoughts as you "think yourself happy" make your day so much better and more pleasant for yourself as well as for the people around you.

Sharing the gospel with a smile has a far greater effect than trying to tell someone of a wonderful way of salvation through a grim, depressed, sour appearance. Everyone is human and has days when they feel a little down and out. You can limit this depression through the strength and power of the Word of God. You may say this is not a temptation, but it is. Satan tempts with means to kill, steal, and destroy. Depression can do all three. Depression steals your joy and kills your testimony. It will utterly destroy you physically as well as mentally and spiritually.

God offers strength and comfort in all matters if we consider Him first in our lives. You may say that someone else doesn't know how you feel or may not have gone through what you have. That may be true, but Christ has. He was tempted in all ways and understands the burdens and trials of your heart. He knows and He cares. He has provided all that we need, so have faith. He is our hope, our friend, our provider, our salvation, and our Lord.

Thirdly, is the temptation of the *pride of life*.

What does it mean to have pride? According to the principle of Noah Webster, "Pride is the proper respect for one's dignity and worth; excessive self-esteem, pleasure or satisfaction over something done, achieved, or owned." This is well and good, if you don't take it to the extreme. It is good to be aware of oneself as we are made in the image of God. You are God's child, and that is something to be proud of. Jesus loved you enough to give His life that you might live. We should be thankful for the life that God has given us and take care of that life. Our bodies are important; therefore, we should see to it that we keep them healthy. Life itself is precious, and nothing should be administered that could cause harm or illness. Tobacco, alcohol, overeating, not eating enough, drugs, etc., can damage and harm your body. Abstaining from harmful habits can make you healthier, mentally and physically alert to do the will of God. You can be a vibrant servant who will be ready, willing, and able to spread the gospel. I know it is easier said than done, but if you pray, God will help and strengthen your resistance to the temptation.

Physical cleanliness is essential when you associate with the public. No one likes to talk to or be around someone who has an offensive, foul body odor, so keep yourself clean and free from communicable, transmitted diseases that can hinder your service. Be refreshed and ready to do business for the Lord.

Being clean on the outside, however, doesn't make you clean on the inside. Appearance can be very deceiving. You can be appealing to the eyes but have a heart filled with sin. Remember, God looks upon the heart, and nothing is hidden from Him. What you speak reveals the intent of your heart. Being high-minded or thinking that you are superior to someone else is having a proud heart. God hates a proud heart. If a man thinks himself to be something when he is nothing, he deceives himself (Gal. 6:3). Not one person is better than another, for God loves us all, and He has no respect of persons. It doesn't matter what nationality you are, what you look like, how wealthy or poor you may be, or if you are "high tech" or a "redneck," for Jesus gave His life for everyone.

Another aspect of pride is self-pride, which can originate with a simple pat on the back.

Satan can tell you how good you are and how much you have accomplished for God that you will begin to listen and build yourself up instead of giving glory to God. Before you realize it, you are setting yourself up on a pedestal, receiving all the honor and recognition and placing God on a shelf. You may be an excellent teacher, pastor, musician, singer, etc.; but give God the praise for your talents and use your talents for His honor and glory. He has given you the ability and has allowed you to minister through these gifts. Remember, the Lord gives and the Lord can take away. We are all special in God's sight no matter what type of job we do for Him. We all work together and make up the body of Christ.

A proud heart is selfish and full of conceit, leaving no room for love or charity. Although you may gain outstanding achievements in this life and many worldly possessions, all these things will be left behind when death knocks at your door. Your possessions will be worthless and cannot be used for bargaining on judgment day. There will be a time when no man shall work, but the end will come. Rejoice if your name is written in the Lamb's Book of Life. Lift God up with praises, and He will see that you receive a just reward. If you accept the glory on earth, you will lose your reward when you stand before the judgment seat of Christ.

All temptations can be suppressed if you:

(1) Recognize the temptation and its source.
(2) Sear the root of the temptation.
(3) Cast the temptation aside.
(4) Replace the temptation with positive words of Christ.

The Spirit of God can enable you to discern the spirits whether they are good or evil (1 Cor. 12:10). Put your trust in God and not man for there are many false prophets in the world who will lead you astray. If you have to think about doing something before you do it, or if you have a question of whether it is right or wrong, more than likely, if it is questionable to begin with, then it is probably wrong. A lot of times, a person will try to justify their actions because they want to do something that they know is contrary to God's will according to the scriptures. They even take scriptures out of context to fit their situation. Do not deceive yourself. Study and meditate on the Word of Truth (2 Tim. 2:15) and let God be in control. Jesus came to give us an abundant life.

CHAPTER 3
CENTER OF GOD'S WILL

The everyday hustle of coming and going, taking care of this and that overshadows the reason for our mere existence. We were born to serve and worship the Lord and to have a relationship with Him and know Him.

In life's scurrying, we tend to hide our mission and purpose in the back of our minds and become too busy to listen to God's instructions. The Bible teaches us that the steps of a righteous man are ordered by the Lord. If we would only stop for a moment and realize that our life here on earth is but for a short span and then eternity begins. Whatever we gain on this earth will pass away, and our salvation and works will determine the reign of our destiny. The materials we have stored, the house we live in, the friends we have, the clothes we wear, and the food we eat will mean nothing when we stand naked before God. Only our hearts will be searched and our deeds recognized. The Bible says to take no heed what you eat or drink or the clothes that you wear, for your Heavenly Father knows what you need and will supply them. Jesus did not have a place to lay His head as He traveled this earth, but His mission was accomplished. It's not wrong to have material things, but it's OK if you can't afford to keep up with the Joneses. God wants you to be blessed, not for selfish gain, but for you to be able to share with others in need.

Many Christians ask, "How do you know if you are in God's will or what is God's will for your life?" Having a clean heart and mind, trusting Him, and obeying His Word is His will. If you don't take time to listen to God's voice, you will never know His will for your life.

I realize that you have responsibilities in general living to provide for your family. If you take or make time for God first, you will find that everything else will fall into place. You can always find an excuse for not spending time in prayer or meditation in God's Word. God has given so much; we surely can make the sacrifice of a little time for Him.

Being a dedicated Christian is more than just going to church on Sunday morning for a couple of hours, eating lunch, and going home. You can surely do that and need to, but your life for Christ will have no fulfillment. When trouble or heartaches come, you will wonder why it has happened to you or wonder where God is.

His will is for you to help win souls. The Holy Ghost gives you the power to become a witness (Acts: 1:8). The more you tell your story of how God saved you and changed your life, the easier it will be to share with others.

A recent hospitalization has shown me that you need to make the best of every situation that comes. No matter where you are, God can speak to your heart and give you strength to do His will. He allows things to happen to you in order for His glory to be manifested. Though suffering may come, you can trust that all will be well. While I was in the hospital, hooked to an IV pole, God gave me the opportunity to talk to another patient about Jesus. As I was walking down the hall to help get my strength back, I passed by another patient's room. The Holy Spirit spoke to my heart to talk to the lady. Through obedience, God blessed and encouraged the lady with His Word, and that in turn blessed me. It will give you a feeling of satisfaction to encourage someone else and to know that you are trying your best to please the Lord.

Sometimes we tend to be selfish and want selfish gain in our lives, thinking only of ourselves. We focus on our own desires. When we seek God first and His righteousness, the other things in life will be given to us (Matt. 6:33).

Education is good, and investing is necessary for planning for the future as long as you keep your priorities in order. It is wise to ask God for guidance. The famous quote "Father Knows Best" is a true statement. Your Heavenly Father knows what you need even before you ask Him. His Word is a lamp unto our feet, and a light unto our path (Ps. 119:105). We see more clearly when we are led by Him.

I believe His will is based on two commandments: (1) Love God and (2) Love your neighbor as yourself. If you love God with all your heart, mind, soul, and strength, the second commandment will come easy. Preferring your brother to yourself and seeing his or her needs will become more important than your own selfishness. Helping someone else will bring showers of blessings to you from God. You will notice that if you pray for someone else's healing, your healing will also come. Your needs will be met before you even realize it.

I believe that each person has a purpose in this life. God has chosen each one who believes and accepts Him to fulfill a work. Each work is to glorify God. He has given talents and gifts in order for us to have an opportunity to bring others to the knowledge of Jesus. We are on a mission to preach, teach, and show others that God is the only true and living God and Jesus Christ is His only Begotten Son.

Jesus went about doing good deeds, helping, and healing. Don't you believe this is what God wants us to do, to be Christlike? It's all about Him and not about us. Why would you think that God's will for your life would be for your own recognition? Satan was cast out of heaven because of wanting selfish recognition, to be like God. Think about the fruits of the Spirit. They are not "high and mighty" but are centered around meekness and gentleness.

God's will for our life is to show love, spread peace, be long-suffering, have faith and self-control, and to do good unto all men bearing one another's burdens. We are taught in His Word to visit the sick, minister to those in prison, help your neighbor, clothe the naked, feed the hungry, and love your enemies.

You may say, "That sounds like too much work." If your heart is right with God, doing these things will become a way of life, and you will find joy being in the center of God's will as you share the gospel to all mankind.

CHAPTER 4

FEAR—POWERS OF DARKNESS

One of the most potent demonic forces against the believer is *fear*. This chapter tells of true encounters of the power of darkness and the demonic accomplices of intimidation and humiliation.

Time seemed to stand still as I watched for the breaking of day. My eyes squinted in the darkness trying to see a small flicker of light through the tightly drawn blinds against the windowsill of my bedroom. Glancing from my bed to the dimly lit hallway and across the room, I could see only shadows in the darkness.

I sensed something was wrong but didn't know exactly what. I had a strange feeling that I was not alone. Was I dreaming? No, I knew I was awake. I kept looking in the darkness, still feeling that someone was near, then I felt the presence of a being lay upon my breasts. The feeling was so heavy it made breathing difficult. Being gripped with fear, a whisper could not part my lips. I tried to push it away, but there was nothing physically there. Trapped in a zone of terror and with sickness arising in my innermost being, I wanted to scream. I was unable to make a sound.

Oh God, don't let this be happening to me! My eyes were wide open as I tried to see this thing, but there was nothing but hot breath upon my face, and a taunting laughter pounding in my head. I fought helplessly against this presence. The heaviness of a spirit bound my body to the point that not even a muscle could twitch. Whatever it was held me captive. Time seemed endless. Confused and desperate, I couldn't even cry. It was as if I was paralyzed. Why couldn't I call for help? Why was I so weak and unable to conquer this being that had control of my mind and body?

Groping with all my strength, I realized that this being was much stronger than me. *Please, someone help me! Please, make this go away!* As my mind raced frantically to find reality, I thought about demonic powers, but it had never entered my mind that they were real. From within my soul, I could hear the words, *Speak the name of Jesus. There is power in the name of Jesus. This being cannot have control of you if you plead the blood of Jesus.*

Weakly, but with a trace of faith, I muttered the words, *Jesus, Jesus* in my thoughts. I pled the blood of Jesus. *Be gone from me in Jesus's name.* As I kindled more faith, I felt the being lose his grip on me. A little stronger now, with more faith, I spoke more boldly, and he left as suddenly as he came.

I tried to catch my breath, still afraid to move. Tired and confused, I lay quiet, looking around for a glimpse of anything that made sense. Still afraid to get out of bed, I listened for any sound in the house. My grandson was sleeping quietly in the next room, and the house was as usual. I was so afraid that I could not even sit up. I was afraid that it would come back. I could not believe that this had happened. I somehow could not rid the awful, gruesome feeling that was left in my mind and upon my body of the being that had visited me.

The feeling of being alone and no one even knowing what was happening was the most terrifying and hopeless situation I had ever experienced. It was true. There are demonic powers wanting to destroy your mind and manipulate you with fear.

Thank God for His amazing power and for His goodness.

It was a long time before I was finally able to proceed with daily living without the fear of being alone, especially at night. I didn't want to ever think about it again, so I never spoke about the episode to anyone. I kept it to myself.

Every day I rekindled my faith and realized that God is more powerful than anyone or anything in heaven and on earth. I thought that I would never have to deal with another encounter again. This was not true. In a few days, I was aroused from sleep again. This time, I was not alone. My husband was lying next to me, and I thought that I was safe and secure. Again, fear gripped my soul without warning. I could not speak, and when I tried to reach out to my husband, I could not move. I tried to cry, but not a whimper would come forth just like before. My mind was racing from thought to thought searching for what I should do.

Surely, my husband can feel this thing like I can and will make it go away, but he was sleeping quietly. My only hope was in Jesus. Again, I pled the blood of Jesus, and the feeling left promptly. When I recovered my sanity with tears streaming down my face, I awakened my husband and told him what had happened. He comforted me and told me that I wasn't crazy and I was not the only one who had visitations. He had once had an encounter himself but had never told anyone. He said it was a cold, bone-chilling presence he had encountered, which left him shivering. The presence did not linger long but was a very uncomfortable feeling.

If it had been a physical battle or an act of violence, it would have made more sense. This was in my spirit. My mind had little control and only thought patterns that raced with confusion searching diligently for reality. I felt so alone not knowing how to take control of what was happening.

Thank God I had enough of the Spirit of God to know where my only help would come from. Within myself, I was powerless, and without God, I would not have a sane mind today.

Unbelievable experiences and encounters with Satan and his demons are no laughing matter or to be brushed off lightly. Well, you may say, "I don't believe that," or "That was just a dream." Be careful what you say. You might have to eat your words tonight.

Powers of darkness are real and controlling. Tactics of fear will grope and control you to the point that it will overtake your sanity. People are unaware of the depth of darkness that sin can take you. Practicing witchcraft only touches the realm. It is not make-believe or tales someone has made up. It is nothing to play with like a game. The certainty that Satan is real is not a fanatical statement. He wants to destroy you. He has some nasty boys to help him.

Demons were defeated when Jesus was resurrected and took the keys of death, hell, and the grave. It is not God's will for fear to be in control. Jesus stated in the Word (2 Tim. 1:7) that God does not give us the spirit of fear but of power, love, and a sound mind. Reading the Word and praying daily will bring you closer to God, and your growth spiritually will help to conquer the destructiveness of Satan.

Your mind needs to be fed with the Word of God, for His Spirit dwells within. Submit yourselves to God, resist the devil, and he will flee from you (James 4:7). Draw close to God, and He will draw close to you (James 4:8). The name of Jesus puts demons to flight, and His overcoming power is the only resource. His Word is our weapon, and the armor of God is our strength.

The experiences taught me that I am only a branch, and that Jesus is the vine (John 15:5–7). If I am not attached to the vine, I have no strength and no ability to face the powers of darkness that are loosed on earth.

Satan can come to you in many ways, but your mind is the center of control. Whatever enters the mind is transferred to the heart. Whether it is fear, doubt, loneliness, despair, sickness, or whether it is faith, joy, happiness, or hope, it is centered in your mind.

Having a Pentecostal background, I have seen unexplained happenings in the church. A lot of people ridicule and mock the Pentecostal churches, but I have found some very devout Christian people in a Pentecostal church.

True Christians that have a deep personal relationship with God pray effectual prayers. I know that in all denominations, you have true believers and some hypocrites. That's another story. Getting back to the unexplained happenings, my family and I are first-hand witnesses to demons being cast out of people. Not made-up stories, but we witnessed it with our own eyes. This was an awesome experience, but nothing to play with. You have heard the phrase "Don't try this at home"—well, I would advise you not to look for demons to cast out. In other words, "don't go looking for trouble." You might find more than you bargained for.

As I recall, a young lady was brought to the altar for prayer. As the pastor and elders of the church began to pray for her, we noticed her countenance change before our very own eyes. She turned her head slowly looking at each individual around her. Her eyes were like fire and seemed to pierce your very soul as she looked straight into your eyes. It made you shudder just to look at her. She straightened herself and seemed to tower over you, and her voice deepened as she began to speak with a man's voice instead of a young teenage girl's. Two well-developed adult men held her as she tried to break loose. She then began struggling with so much strength that it was all the two men could do to hold her. She tried to bite the people that were standing around her gnashing her teeth, cursing and slashing out at the pastor. She looked as though she was so full of hate and, with a deep, hoarse voice, cried out, "She's mine, and you can't have her."

Her neck began to swell, and the necklace she was wearing began to tighten more and more. Her face began changing colors. The necklace would have choked her if someone hadn't broken and released it. After fervent prayer and rebuking those demons in the name of Jesus, she screamed a horrifying scream as foam dripped from her mouth, and then she became limp. The demons had torn from her body and left her lying on the floor. The elders carried her to the pew, and she lay there quietly as she renewed her strength. She stood even though she was still very weak and confessed Jesus as Lord. She was instructed to keep herself cleansed by the Word and live for the Lord, or more demons could come in to her, and she would be worse than she was.

I had never witnessed anything like this. It was as though she was a different person. She transformed from a sweet, friendly, young lady to someone who was horrible, unremorseful, vile, full of hate, cursing, and fighting.

Logically, how can a person's neck swell so fast and then go back to normal in a matter of minutes? How can a man's voice come from a frail, small-framed teenage girl? How can she have the strength of two men?

It's amazing how a spirit can take over your body, but more amazing how Jesus has more power and can deliver you from such. I John 4:4 says greater is He that is in you than he that is in the world. Happenings like this cannot be explained because they are spiritual, not physical.

I have seen and heard many instances of devils being cast out and spiritual encounters that people have had.

In a church in LaGrange, I witnessed a demon cast out of a young woman. Foam flowed from her mouth as she writhed on the floor and screamed as she was delivered.

I know of an experience involving a very young girl and her mother. The mom was awakened by the presence of a demonic being. The vision that the woman saw was a terrifying being with red eyes. The being stood over her only for a second. The woman felt in her spirit that something was wrong with her daughter even though she had not heard a sound from her room. The woman ran to the daughter's room and found her crying and struggling for breath. The daughter began frantically telling her mom that there were demons all around her. The mom saw nothing. She called for her husband to come, and they began to pray until the daughter said that the demons were gone.

A teenager, whom I have confidence in, once told me that she had a hair-raising experience one night. She had gone somewhere and, on the way home, had car trouble. She got out of the car and began to walk to a nearby telephone booth. As she was walking, she heard someone walking behind her. She told me she was so frightened because when she turned around, there was no one there. As she made a step, she could hear rustling behind her. She began walking faster, and she felt a breath blowing against her hair. She made it to the telephone and called home. She said she never saw anyone, but she would never forget that feeling.

You may say that I have a vivid imagination or have watched too many movies. Well, I don't even watch scary movies. If you have never experienced things of this nature, you may not believe or understand. Don't say that it will never happen to you, for it might. If it does, be prepared in the name of Jesus.

People seem to think that demons are not real and witchcraft is only practiced in Haiti or some other foreign country. Do you know that satanic churches may be in your own town or county? People who worship Satan could be your next-door neighbor.

The end-time is close at hand, and Satan is trying his best to get you. Don't sit in ignorance, but open your eyes to the truth. We don't wrestle against flesh and blood but against spiritual powers of darkness (Eph. 6:12).

Fear can grope you in many ways in unexpected times. Most of the time, it is when you are alone, but it can happen when you are in a crowd. Fear has no respect of day or night. I remember one day in my own home as I was cleaning the bathroom, I heard a baby crying as if they were hurting. My husband was in the basement watching TV. The cry was so heartbreaking I ran to the door and asked if he was watching a movie with a baby in it. He said no, and he did not hear it.

I returned to my cleaning, and suddenly a baby doll of my daughter's fell off the tub, and her head came off. That was certainly weird and made me think twice.

Another time, I was making our bed when out of the corner of my eye, I saw the swinging light on the other side of the bed began swinging. I looked up, and it kept swinging. Nevertheless, I finished making the bed quickly. Then I heard a voice of a child call out "Mama" from my daughter's playroom. Of course, no one was there. I thought, *My mind is playing tricks on me. It's just because I'm alone in this big house, and I don't like to be alone.* Who knows? Bizarre things do happen that no one can explain.

Whether demonic powers tease you or fear tries to creep into your mind, we have to grow in the Word and power through Jesus to fight against the evil that is loosed on earth.

The disciples were unable to cast some demons out for Jesus taught in Mark 9:29 that some are cast out only through much prayer and fasting.

I am thankful that I know a risen Lord and Savior who can do miracles on this earth. He not only can cast out demons, but He can also heal the sick. Doctors stand in awe when they cannot explain how someone can be healed, and a cancer or a tumor miraculously disappear with no logical answer. You will find no answers in the world about the mysteries of God, for it "confounds the wise." Our minds cannot comprehend the awesomeness of our Heavenly Father, His only Begotten Son, Jesus, and the Holy Ghost of God.

Whether it is fear from Satan, fear of failing, or phobias in daily living, we can put our trust in God and know His grace is sufficient for our every need. He loves and cares for us. We don't need to lean on our own understanding, but we need to acknowledge Him, and lean on Him for guidance and direction in all we see and do.

Satan tries to make you anxious, worried, and dread. Every time people hear a siren or get a call in the middle of the night, the first impulse is to immediately think of the worst possible scenario. First thoughts of fear are always negative, and there is no age limit for fear. I remember when I was a child, I was so afraid of storms. Mainly, because my grandmother was afraid and would get us up, especially at night, and make us sit in a little hallway on an old trunk till the storm passed by. Of course, we had drop lights, which hung from the high ceiling ending in a lightbulb. The bulbs would pop sometimes when lightning struck close.

As I grew older, during a daytime storm, I would sit and read the Bible. I was not a Christian at that time, but somehow when I read the scriptures, they gave me peace during the storm.

If you tend to get nervous or become afraid, try singing. Gospel music of worship and praise will set the atmosphere for serenity. When fearful thoughts enter your mind, try saying to yourself, *God, you have this, I trust you.* Even when bad things happen, you have the assurance that God is with you through it all. Putting your focus on God brings delight to Him and puts joy in your heart. We are sheltered in the arms of God. He is our refuge and hiding place. He is our strong tower and present help in times of trouble.

CHAPTER 5

OVERCOMING POWER

The longer you serve Christ and develop a close relationship, living for Him will become easier. Old bad habits can be replaced by good habits. Everyone needs help when it comes to controlling the tongue. The Holy Spirit can give you power to overcome quick tempers and harsh words. You will be able to show love instead of retaliation. You can learn to be humble and kind.

The Bible teaches us to love one another and, if it be possible, live peaceably with all men (Rom. 12:18). You can learn to control your actions and what you say if you listen to the Spirit. God has given us so much grace and extended mercy to us. We in turn should show mercy and grace to others. This takes time as you grow in the Lord. You can learn to be patient, forgiving, and think of others, becoming less selfish.

Isaiah 53:5 states, "He was wounded for our transgressions, he was bruised for our iniquities: the chastisement of our peace was upon Him; and with His stripes we are healed." Jesus made a way by overcoming every obstacle. We can be enriched by overcoming power through His name.

Without God we are powerless, but with God we can tread on serpents and take authority in His name. I can do all things through Christ who strengthens me (Phil. 4:13). Jesus is so powerful and greatly to be praised. May we give eternal glory to God, our Heavenly Father. "No weapon that is formed against thee shall prosper" (Isa. 54:17).

Many battles were fought in the Old Testament. The Israelites won the battle when they put God first, but lost when they turned from Him and were disobedient. Learn from these lessons and know that it is not by might, nor by power, but by the Spirit of the Lord of Hosts (Zechariah 4:6).

There is none greater than God Almighty. Nothing or no one on earth or in heaven is greater. Jesus won the battle when He rose from the dead on the third day. He took the keys of hell and death (Rev. 1:18) and has all authority and power. You may have to contend with criticism and unbelievers may ridicule or make fun of you, but rejoice because your name is written in the Book of Life.

Being a child of God is so awesome knowing that He is your deliverer and King. Nothing will befall you that He doesn't know about or allows. If He allows something to come your way, He has made a way for you to escape or overcome. He loves you and will take care of you. Through Him, you live, move, and have your being. He has given you benefits and promises if you will endure to the end and trust in Him. Be an overcomer and a living vessel that God can use to bring Him glory.

We can't imagine the rewards that are laid up for the Christian who stands true to Him. Can you fathom no problems, troubles, worries, sadness, death, sickness, pain, fear, and no tears? Only goodness and mercy shall follow the believer and abundant life everlasting in a mansion built by God himself. There will be no darkness for Christ will be the light. There will be no need for bars or locks on the doors or windows to keep robbers and thieves out. Only those who have been redeemed by the blood of the Lamb will be permitted to dwell. Joy and happiness for eternity sounds good, doesn't it?

After judgment on earth, a new heaven and a new earth will come down. There will be singing and praising God in a place of tranquility and peace. It will be like the garden of Eden, where you can walk and talk with the Lord in the cool of the day.

My prayer for you is to keep growing in the Lord. Keep your eyes on Him and don't look back. Be focused on your destination of where you are going and not where you came from. Work now, for the time is coming when there will be no more work to do, for heaven and earth as we know it will pass away. Be strong in the Lord and turn your back when temptation comes. Jesus has overcome the world, and you can too through Him. Be like a tree that is planted by the rivers of water, where your roots can grow deep in the good soil of God's Word. Read the Word slowly and meditate on it. Whenever the storms come, get grounded in the Word and stand firm in the power of God. Let His Spirit abide in you to teach and guide you in the ways of the Lord. You can live a triumphant life if you trust and seek Him.

The best is yet to come, for Jesus is coming back to get His children (born-again Christians) out of this sin-sick world. Live each day as though it was your last. Life is short, so spread the gospel to the world and look and listen for the trump of God to sound. If we go by the grave or by the rapture, we will be with the Lord.

ABOUT THE AUTHOR

Patsy Hamil, locally known as "Miss Patsy" is quite a character though small in stature. Her energy, humor, and teasing is contagious. Having a deep relationship with Jesus, she expresses love and compassion to everyone she meets, adults and children alike.

Although elderly, she continues to be a witness for "Christ and enjoys working in the community. She strongly supports attending church services and fellowship with believers. "Miss Patsy" works for the Senior Center delivering meals on wheels five days a week to shut-ins.

Through the years, she has given her time and talent to be pianist and organist for many churches. She is well known for her foot stomping music. She has performed duties as Sunday School teacher for adults and children, family training hour teacher, gospel singer, choir leader, church clerk, secretary, and treasurer for the women's ministry.

"Miss Patsy" has authored a children's book entitled "Let's Go to Church" and is currently in the process of publishing a book of inspired poetry.

Her greatest desire is to encourage people to give their heart to God and put Him first in their life and to love one another.

Printed in the United States
by Baker & Taylor Publisher Services